A HISTORY OF QUAKERS
IN PEMBROKESHIRE

As this third impression is being published in the year of Waldo Williams' centenary, we include one of his most popular poems, translated by D.M.Lloyd.

REMEMBERING

One blissful moment as the sun is setting,
A mellow moment ere the night comes on,
To bring to mind things which are long forgotten,
Now lost in dust of eras that are gone.

Now like the foam breaking on lonely beaches,
Or the wind's song and no one there to hear,
I know they call on us to listen,-
The old forgotten things men loved so dear.

Things wrought through cunning skill in early ages,
Neat little dwellings and resplendent halls,
And well-told stories that are lost forever,
And olden gods on whom no suppliant calls.

The little words of languages once living,
Lively was then their sound on lips of men,
And pleasing to the ear in children's prattle,
But now, no tongue will fashion them again.

O countless generations of earth's children,
Of dreams divine, and fragile godlikeness,
Is there but stillness for the hearts that quickened,
That knew delight and knew grief's bitterness?

Often when evening falls and I am lonely
I long once more to bring you all to mind,
Pray, is there no-one treasures and holds dear
The old forgotten things of humankind?

COFIO

Un funud fach cyn elo'r haul o'r wybren,
    Un funud fwyn cyn delo'r hwyr i'w hynt,
I gofio am y pethau anghofiedig
    Ar goll yn awr yn llwch yr amser gynt.

Fel ewyn ton a dyr ar draethell unig,
    Fel cân y gwynt lle nid oes glust a glyw,
Mi wn eu bod yn galw'n ofer arnom-
    Hen bethau anghofiedig dynol ryw.

Camp a chelfyddyd y cenhedloedd cynnar,
    Anheddau bychain a neuaddau mawr,
Y chwedlau cain a chwalwyd ers canrifoedd
    Y duwiau na ŵyr neb amdanynt 'nawr.

A geiriau bach hen ieithoedd diflanedig,
    Hoyw yng ngenau dynion oeddynt hwy,
A thlws I'r glust ym mharabl plant bychain,
    Ond tafod neb ni eilw arnynt mwy.

O, genedlaethau direfedi daear,
    A'u breuddwyd dwyfol a'u dwyfoldeb brau,
A erys ond tawelwch I'r calonnau
    Fu gynt yn llawenychu a thristáu?

Mynych ym mrig yr hwyr, a mi yn unig,
    Daw hiraeth am eich nabod chwi bob un;
A oes a'ch deil o hyd mewn cof a chalon,
    Hen bethau anghofiedig teulu dyn?

WALDO WILLIAMS (in Dail Pren, Gomer)

A History of Quakers in Pembrokeshire

Stephen Griffith

First Impression - 1990
Second Impression - 1995
Third Impression - 2004

ISBN 0 9546991 0 6

© Stephen Griffith

Printed by Gomer Press, Llandysul, Dyfed.

CONTENTS

NOTE FOR THE THIRD IMPRESSION.

Fourteen years have passed since the publication of the first edition of "The History of Quakers in Pembrokeshire"; but history has not stayed still.

We are now planning an extension to the Meeting House at Milford Haven, and to bring it into the 21st Century. Since its age has given it special status, as a listed building, we are careful to maintain the main structure intact, with its American design of 1811.

As with other organisations, membership of the Meeting at Milford Haven has also seen many changes since the first edition was published. English is still the language of the Meeting for Worship, but Welsh is used wherever appropriate.

We feel the loss of Waldo Williams, a former member, whose fame as a Welsh poet reverberates throughout Wales; he was an example to us all. Waldo was born in Haverfordwest in 1904. We are helping to celebrate his life and work at a special centenary exhibition, from September 19th to October 1st 2004, at the beautiful exhibition hall attached to Haverfordwest County Library. We will be joined by prominent poets, speakers and soloists. Over 50 artists in the area have promised to produce special pieces for this exhibition.

Keeping up with modern technology, we have now established a web site (www.quakersin pembrokeshire.org.uk) giving details of our meetings in Milford Haven, Narberth, and St David's, together with background information about Quakerism.

We are peacemakers and trust that the will of God may guide us to build a more peaceful world.

Stephen Griffith
January 2004

PREFACE

This short history of Quakers in Pembrokeshire is being published by Friends from Milford Haven Preparative Meeting to mark the bi-centenary anniversary of the town. Friends are grateful to Stephen Griffith for his painstaking research and attention to detail in producing this book.

The original manuscript was prepared for Quakers in South Wales, but this printed edition includes an introduction which will help to make it appreciated by a wider readership.

Members of the Meeting would like to thank Dyfed Elis-Gruffydd for the photograph of the Meeting House, the Quaker Tapestry Group for the use of the photograph of the Milford tapestry on the front cover, Miss Dilys Williams for permission to reproduce the poem 'Mewn Dau Gae' by her brother, and Penguin Publications Limited for permission to reproduce the translation.

Signed on behalf of Milford Haven Preparative Meeting.

Kay Allen, Clerk
September 1990

INTRODUCTION

The story of Quakers in Pembrokeshire is unique in the history of the Society of Friends.

Although seven Meeting Houses existed in 1682 persistent persecution led many Quakers to emigrate to the New World. By 1792 only one meeting house, at Haverfordwest, was officially listed.

Then, in an unusual reversal of history, American Quakers came to Milford Haven, started a whaling industry, and eventually, in 1811, constructed a Meeting House, the only meeting house ever built in this country by Americans. When the Americans left the area the Society again declined. However, in 1990, there is a flourishing Meeting at Milford Haven and smaller groups meet elsewhere in Pembrokeshire. Quakerism is expanding again.

This history has been carefully researched by Stephen Griffith, an Elder of Milford Haven Meeting, and a Quaker for forty years. Stephen was born in North Wales but came to live in Neyland in 1949, when he joined the staff of Pembroke Grammar School. He is a member of the Gorsedd and has written several short books and articles in Welsh.

Readers who are not members of the Society will need to know a little of its history and organisation in order to appreciate the text.

Quakerism began in the seventeenth century, a period of passionate interest in religion. Many were dissatisfied with the worldliness and hypocrisy of the churchmen of the day and turned to what they saw as a revival of primitive Christianity, a mystical religion of great simplicity. George Fox (1624-1691), one of the greatest of Christian mystics, a man of enormous faith, vision and charisma, helped to co-ordinate these scattered groups and bring them together into the Society of Friends. George Fox visited Pembrokeshire and is mentioned in the text. (Late in life he married Margaret Fell, widow of a judge on the northern circuit who had always been sympathetic to Quakerism. She is also mentioned in the text.)

In about 1654 some of the most devoted followers of George Fox were sent out across the country to hold meetings explaining Quaker beliefs, and to bring together those sympathetic to the new sect. In Quaker history they are known as the 'Valiant Sixty'.

Several of the 'Valiant Sixty' came to Pembrokeshire. Thomas Holme, the first Quaker mentioned as visiting Pembrokeshire probably came in about 1654. He was a weaver from Kendal. His wife, Elizabeth, visited Pembrokeshire in 1659 (she had suffered greatly when trying to convert students in Oxford). John Burnyeat, a husbandman from Crabtree Beck, made several visits commencing, as far as is known, in 1667.

One of the first Welsh Quakers was John ap John, also mentioned in the text. John ap John was a native of Wrexham and was a follower of Morgan Llwyd, a notable preacher. When Llwyd heard of George Fox he sent John ap John and another of his followers to listen to him and to report back. John ap John went but did not return; instead he became a Quaker.

Quaker church government, also mentioned in the text, needs to be understood. It is very simple. Each Meeting (the equivalent of a church) holds a business meeting once a month. At this Preparative Meeting, representatives are appointed to a Monthly Meeting where members from meetings in a particular county or area discuss current concerns. A Yearly Meeting gathers representatives from all Meetings in a larger area, usually a country. In the past there have been intermediate meetings between monthly and yearly meetings known as Quarterly Meetings.

General Meetings are occasionally held to draw together people from several areas.

Friends have always been active in social reform. Despite relatively small numbers they have played a significant part in pioneering developments in the abolition of slavery, the erection of mental hospitals, universal education, famine relief, working conditions in industry, temperance, and in many other areas but perhaps especially in the field of pacifism.

Waldo Williams who died in 1971, was one of the best known members of Milford Haven Meeting, although few knew of his Quaker convictions. He was a much loved Welsh poet of great distinction.

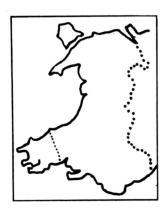

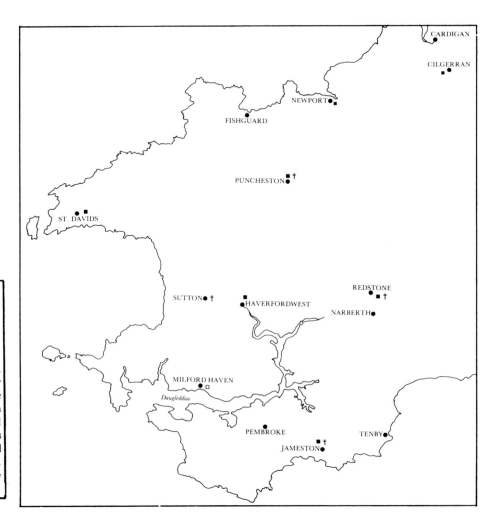

CARDIGAN

CILGERRAN ■

NEWPORT ● ■

FISHGUARD ●

PUNCHESTON ■ †
●

ST. DAVIDS ● ■

REDSTONE
● ■ †

SUTTON ● †

HAVERFORDWEST ■
●

NARBERTH ●

MILFORD HAVEN ●
□

Daugleddau

PEMBROKE ●

JAMESTON ■ †
●

TENBY ●

Chapter One

THE FIRST QUAKERS

Quakers came to Pembrokeshire in the seventeenth century. Thomas Holme, a weaver from Kendal, and one of the 'Valiant Sixty', wrote to Margaret Fell:

> The last week I was in Pembrokeshire. It's called 'Litte England beyond Wales'. The most of that County is English. The Lord hath a people there. In Tenby, which stands upon the edge of the sea, I had five meetings. Four of them I had at the mayor's house, and the other at his brother's ... I lay four nights in the mayor's house, and a Welshman with me [almost certainly John ap John, one of the first Welsh Quakers] I took along, which is serviceable.
>
> We passed to Pembroke town. In that town there is one alderman convinced, and a shoe-maker too.
>
> And from thence we passed to Haverfordwest, the greatest town in Wales, and there a merchant of the town [almost certainly William Bateman] is convinced. And we got a meeting that night of near two hundred people at his house in that town. [1]

In 1657, George Fox [2] journeyed, in the company of John ap John, through South Wales to Pembrokeshire. The two men were warmly greeted by the mayor and one of the justices of Tenby. But, as was his custom, John ap John went into the 'steeple-house' (a Quaker nickname for the church); and because he refused to doff his hat 'the governor cast him into prison'. There followed an interesting discussion between George Fox and the governor of the prison. Fox asked him why he had cast his friend into prison:

'For standing with his hat on in the church.'

'Had not the priest two caps on his head, a black one and a white one? Cut off the brim of the hat and then my friend would have but one, and the brim of the hat were only to save the rain from his neck.'

'These are frivolous things,' said the governor.

'Why then,' said Fox, 'dost thou cast my friend into prison for such frivolous things?'

John ap John was released and Fox was invited to dine at the governor's house.

On the departure of the two friends from Tenby, they were escorted by the mayor and his wife, a justice and his wife and several others for half a mile out of town, and they held a prayer-meeting on the beach.

Fox does not mention in his Journal places which he visited in Pembrokeshire, other than Pembroke and Haverfordwest, where he was welcomed and had a 'great meeeting'.

Before long, the Quakers were holding meetings regularly in Jameston (near Manorbier), Haverfordwest, Redstone (near Llanddewi Felffre), St. Davids, Newport, Puncheston, and possibly Cilgerran, and there were burial grounds associated with the Meeting Houses at Jameston, Haverfordwest, Redstone and Puncheston. The Pembroke County Monthly Meetings[3] were held regularly either at Redstone or Haverfordwest. And it was at Redstone that the first Yearly Meeting for Wales was held in 1682.

The Quakers of Pembrokeshire were visited by Richard Davies,[4] an enthusiastic missionary from Welshpool. According to his manual, 'An account of the convincement, exercises, services and travels', he came to Puncheston twice. The first time was in 1665 and after journeying on his own from Gloucestershire and Worcestershire, he held services at Redstone and Haverfordwest:

> The last I had was at Puncheston among the Welsh; they having notice of a Welshman coming to keep a meeting in those parts, many came to that meeting, and good service I had for the Lord, the truth being declared in their own language to them. We had the meeting out of doors, and I stood with my back towards the wall of Thomas Simmons' house. I was young and strong and my voice was heard to the steeple-house, and most of them came out to see me; and only a few came out with the priest when he had done ... I was informed that the priest's wife and daughters were at the meeting, and were very loving and tender, and came to be convinced of the truth ...

Richard Davies' second journey to Puncheston in 1668 in the company of a Friend, Thomas Ellis of Dolgellau, was an unpleasant experience. As they did not start from Cardigan town until late in the day, night came upon them and their guide lost his way; and in the rain '. . . we wandered up and down among the peat or turf-pits, and other dangerous places, but the Lord preserved us out of them all'. They reached Puncheston at dead of night and were welcomed by Thomas Simmons.

The 'first publishers of truth', as the early Quakers called themselves, had a satisfying response from the inhabitants of Pembrokeshire.[5] John Burnyeat, another of the 'Valiant Sixty', in the company of John ap John came to the county in 1667, 1668, 1669, 1675, and 1676. Elizabeth Holme (wife of Thomas Holme) and Alice Burkett, also from England, preached in 'large meetings' in Haverfordwest in 1659, and Hugh Roberts from Pennsylvania, held a preaching mission to Haverfordwest and Redstone, in 1697.

Relatively few Quakers in Pembrokeshire were gaoled during Cromwell's Republic, although the Puritans who had been granted freedom to worship by Charles I were unwilling to extend that right to other Nonconformists when Cromwell came to rule.

When Fox was arrested in 1654 and sent to London, he and Cromwell had a long conversation; and at the end of their discussion Cromwell said to him: 'Come again to my house, for if thou and I were but an hour a day together, we should be nearer one to the other.' Cromwell died on 3 September, 1658.

Although Cromwell himself was not unfriendly, there are records of the imprisonment of Friends in Pembrokeshire during the Republic; viz John ap John, James Jones (Haverfordwest), William Thomas (Llanddewi Felffre), Elizabeth Holme and Alice Burkett.

However, during the thirty years following the death of Cromwell, no day passed without the presence of a Quaker in the prison at Haverfordwest.[6] The Society of Friends kept a fairly accurate account of the suffering during the seventeenth and eighteenth century in 'The Collection of the Sufferings'.

In August, 1661, Lewis David and his wife Susan, James Lewis, Alice Lewis, Evan John and William Thomas, all from Llanddewi Felffre, were put in Haverfordwest prison for refusing to keep away from Meetings for Worship. About the same time, Thomas Simmons, his wife Jane and their three sons Hugh, John and Evan, from Puncheston, were taken to Haverfordwest prison together with Ursula Simmons, Lawrence Edward, David Edward and Margaret Edward. They were treated very cruelly.[7] They were forced to share a cell with murderers and felons who '... took away their food, pickt their pockets and many ways abused them. The hardships they endured in Winter for want of Fire, having no Place to make any in, was very pinching to several of them, who were both aged and sickly, and had their Hands and Feet much swelled and their bodies looking black. This they endured two Winters, and after about Eighteen Months Imprisonment they were brought to Trial at the Assizes, where the Evidence against them was found insufficient to convict them of being at the Meeting for which they were indicted; wherefore the jury acquitted them, and they were speedily after discharged from their long unjust Confinement'.

On 21 September 1661, William Bateman[8] and his wife Sarah, James Jones, Henry Relief and his wife Elizabeth were caught at a Meeting for Worship at Haverfordwest, and as they refused to agree to non-attendance at such meetings they were put in prison and kept there till the assizes a year later. The men were fined £5 each and the women five marks each, and as they refused to pay were sent to Bridewell Prison in London, except for William Bateman who had his goods distrained to the value of £5.

About the same time, Edmund Williams, David Simmons, John Howell and Richard Poole were caught at a Meeting in William Bateman's house. Three of them were sent to the 'House of Correction' and Richard Poole was ordered to remain in prison '... 'til the Wind served to send him to Ireland, where he dwelt, and then to be whipped and sent thither'.

On 8 September 1662, James Picton was committed to Carmarthen Castle for refusing to swear allegiance '... and from thence, after four Months, removed to the Gaol at Haverfordwest where he remained prisoner many years'.

An interesting case is that of William Bateman of Haverfordwest. He was a member of a well-known family in Pembrokeshire and his association with the Quakers was conspicuous. Between 1605 and 1750, the office of mayor of Haverfordwest was filled thirteen times by a Bateman, and the office of sheriff of the town and county filled several times by a member of the family. No other name appears as often in either of the lists. William Bateman's activities with the Quakers embarrassed those in judicial authority and the Magistrate's Court dealt more leniently with him than with his fellow Quakers. For, as recorded above, whereas those attending Meeting at the Bateman house were committed to prison for a year, he was only subjected to a fine and his goods distrained to settle it.

Not only was there extensive persecution of Quakers before 1662 but in that year oppressive laws were passed by Parliament, one of them aimed particularly at the Quakers. According to this law the Meetings for Worship of Friends were illegal. Also, for refusing to swear an oath—including allegiance—Quakers were fined £5. The fine was doubled for a second offence and there was a three months imprisonment in the case of refusal to pay. Exile awaited each person who committed the offence a third time.

In 1664, the Law of Meeting Houses (the Conventicle Act), was passed. This prohibited a gathering of more than four people over sixteen years of age, in addition to the family of the house, from worshipping in any building apart from the Parish Church. There would be a fine of £5 or imprisonment for three months for offending once; the fine would be doubled for offending a second time; but for offending a third time, the fine would be £100 or exile overseas for seven years.

In the year 1682, William Penn[9] visited America and returned enthusiastic about establishing a colony for Friends on his land in 'Pennsylvania'. He was anxious to populate the region and he encouraged the Quakers in particular to take advantage of his offer. There was promise of a Welsh Settlement—the Welsh Tract—so that the Welsh could feel at home and preserve their language. There would be freedom to worship as they desired, under a State Law which would be just, enlightened and spiritual.

William Penn's ideas had a warm welcome from many Quakers in Pembrokeshire. Their persecution was at its zenith and the future was dark. Here was a land of dreams beckoning to them, where life could begin afresh in an environment of justice under the rule of the Holy Light within.

One of the first to venture was Lewis Davies of Llanddewi Felffre, who bought 3,000 acres for £60, later selling most of the land to other Friends. Among the buyers were William Howell of Castlebythe, Henry Lewis of Redstone, Evan Roberts of Llanycefn and Maurice Scourfield of Narberth. Henry Lewis became one of the founders of a region in Pennsylvania known as Haverford (now the site of a famous Quaker College). He was also prominent in the development of the region and one of the leaders there. It is uncertain how many Pembrokeshire Friends ventured to cross the Atlantic, but the names St Davids and Narberth in Pennsylvania suggest a representative from diverse corners of the county. One emigrant, Maurice Llewellyn, called his house 'Castlebythe', thus revealing his roots.

The ship *William Galley*[10] started its voyage from Carmarthen towards the end of the seventeenth century, and on board, amongst Friends from Radnorshire, there were some from Pembrokeshire. The charges for passengers were £5 for each person over 12 years of age and £2-10s for each one under twelve; sucklings and furniture up to 20 tons could go free. The head of each family was to pay five shillings and all unmarried persons (with the exception of servants) one shilling each to the ship's surgeon.

What type of person emigrated from Pembrokeshire? In the incomplete list of Glenn's *Welsh Founders of Pennsylvania*, thirty-five men and women are identified by name.[11] They left Pembrokeshire during the years spanning 1682-1711. Six were classed as 'gentlemen'; presumably, they were of independent means. Seven were husbandmen, three were farmers, one was an emasculator, one a shoemaker, one a minister of religion (obviously not a Quaker), and one a female servant. Some were wives travelling with their husbands (and family), and some were elderly relations. One boy was under-age but went by permission of his parents. It is very likely that the others, not classified by trade, would be knowledgeable about farming. One or two, maybe, returned on short preaching visits, but the vast majority never set foot in Wales again.

The departure of so many Friends was a terrible loss to the Society. When we regard the contributions of some of them to the development of the Welsh Tract, and indeed, to the establishment of

Government in the U.S.A., we realize the extent of loss that Wales suffered by the emigration of these valiant men and women. They had proved themselves to be dependable leaders in their home districts, and if they had had the freedom to develop their ideas and activities, Wales and religion would have, no doubt, benefitted. As early as 1698 the extent of the emigration had shocked the Society of Friends in Wales, and at Yearly Meeting in Rhaeadr that year much sorrow was expressed. They declared that the emigrants had left a vacancy that weakened many Meetings throughout the country, even destroying the life in some. It was true. The breach left by the emigrants was not filled by others.

By the Act of Tolerance, 1689, the Protestants gained the lawful right to a peaceful life. But in spite of the Act, life for Quakers was uneasy during the eighteenth century. The 1689 Act did not allow freedom from the tyranny of the Parish Church and there was much distraint on their property as they refused to pay tithes and rent to the Church. This tyranny lasted well into the nineteenth century.

The destruction of Quakerism in Pembrokeshire proceeded rapidly. During the ten years 1682-1691, three of the Yearly Meetings for Wales were held in Pembrokeshire but only five were held there from 1691-1797. Regular Meetings came to an end in Puncheston in 1725, Newport in 1726, St Davids in 1732, Redstone in 1766 and Jameston in 1777. The eighteenth century was a very bleak period for the Quakers of Pembrokeshire. [12]

Chapter Two

THE AMERICAN REVIVAL

Towards the end of the eighteenth century, however, an unexpected development took place in Pembrokeshire which heartened Friends in the County. In the foregoing chapter Milford Haven is not mentioned. The reason is a simple one: there were only a few cottages on the banks of the Daugleddau and, as far as is known, none of the early pioneers of Quakerism lived in the vicinity.

In 1758, the land upon which Milford and Hakin were built became the property of William Hamilton through his marriage to Catherine Barlow of Slebech. As soon as he set eyes on the Haven, Hamilton began to plan a harbour which would be useful for developing trade with Ireland and America. But whatever he had in mind, had to be postponed on his appointment as 'Envoy Extraordinary to the Court of Naples', an office he held until 1800.[13] Meanwhile, he was able to get a Bill through Parliament in 1790 which authorized him '. . . to make and provide Quays, Docks, Piers and other erections and to establish a Market with proper Roads and Avenues there . . .'

Hamilton appointed, as his agent in Pembrokeshire, his nephew, Charles Francis Greville, the second son of the Earl of Warwick. Although only in his early thirties at that time, he had already represented Warwick in Parliament in 1774 and was returned for the same borough in successive elections until 1784. He was also, at one time, a Lord of the Admiralty, a Lord of Trade and a Treasurer of the Household. He was a Fellow of the Royal Society because of his wide scientific interests. He was thus well qualified to undertake the responsibility of developing the harbour and town of Milford. Catherine Hamilton died in 1782 and a large sum of money became available to Sir William Hamilton (he was knighted in 1782) and this could be used by Greville to proceed with the task facing him.

Greville realized that he would need more than

stones and bricks in founding a new town. He would need commercial development. And for that, Greville turned his attention towards a group of American Quaker whalers from Nantucket Island, whom he hoped to persuade to carry on their trade in the southern seas from his new town.

Because of religious intolerance in England in the seventeenth century a group of Puritans fled first to Holland, and then in 1620, they sailed on the *Mayflower* to New England. By the middle of the century, they and their descendants had settled well into their new country but they became intolerant of the views held by Baptists and Quakers and subjected them to harassment and persecution. Three Quakers, William Robinson, Marmaduke Stevenson and Mary Dyer were executed in Boston, Massachusetts, the men in 1659 and Mary in 1660 for daring to preach in public. (They are known in Quaker history as 'the Boston Martyrs'.)

Life was so intolerable under the Puritans that a group of men, among whom were Quaker associates,[14] bought islands, one of them being Nantucket, from the native Indians who lived there. One of the Quakers who settled in Nantucket

was Nathaniel Starbuck who had emigrated to America from Derby. Peter Folger was another.

But life on Nantucket was difficult because the soil was shallow and unproductive, until, by chance, they discovered that sperm-oil from whales which inhabited the neighbouring waters was in demand as a source of fuel for lighting. (The streets of London were illuminated by lamps burning sperm oil (spermaceti).)

The whaling industry in Nantucket grew at a phenomenal rate and practically all the inhabitants became involved in producing sperm-oil. Whaleboats were built, and sail-makers together with coopers and rope- and candle-makers made a good living. The island population grew and since the majority were Quakers both religion and the economy of the island were under their control.

They prospered until 1775, when the War of Independence broke out. The Nantucketers refused to take part in the war and consequently they were harassed and looted by the American and British navies alike, and their ships were confined to the harbour. By 1783, when the war came to an end, the Nantucketers were in a pitiful state of poverty. In order to try and improve matters some forty families left the island for the mainland port of Dartmouth, Nova Scotia from where they hoped to rebuild their whaling trade. Their main commerce had been with England, and a small number of representatives travelled to London to explore the prospects of establishing a base in Britain.

Greville knew of the Nantucketers and invited them to establish a base on the Daugleddau where he was commissioned to build a town. [15]

It is almost impossible to state categorically how many immigrants responded to Greville's invitation, most of whom arrived in 1792. There is, however, no doubt about the following: Samuel Starbuck (sen.) and Abigail his wife; Timothy Folger and his wife Abial; Samuel Starbuck (jun.), his wife Lucretia and their children; Daniel Starbuck, his wife Alice and their children; Captain Zacchara Bunker, his wife Judith and some of their children; Captain Uriah Bunker (unmarried), Captain Charles Gardner (unmarried?); Captain Elisha Clark, his wife Elizabeth and their children; Captain Gwinn (without his family); Ruth Bunker, a young unattached Nantucketer who applied for membership of the Society of Friends soon after arriving. [16] From reading the diary of Abial Folger (1806-1811) there is reason to believe that her daughter Peggy Grieve and her husband and children came, but not daughters Abial and Sally. But we are less sure about the two Folger sons with wives and children. The list of immigrants quoted in *Whales and Destiny* (Edouard A. Stackpole, Director of the Museum of The Nantucket Historical Association,) contains other names, but we have no means of knowing if they actually arrived. If we include ancillary workers in the whale-oil business: boat builders, sail makers, coopers, carpenters, smiths, *etc.* it is likely that fifty or more immigrants landed in 1792. However, from amongst those who came, many had left Milford by 1806, some returning to Nantucket, others to Dartmouth (Nova Scotia) where the whaling industry was being re-established, whereas whale-fishing voyages from the quays of Milford were not frequent and were getting less so.

Samuel Starbuck (jun.) and his family were the first to arrive in June 1792, and, because of lack of accommodation, were lodged at Haverfordwest. [17] But Charles Greville arranged accommodation for some five families, who arrived in August 1792, at

Robertson Hall some two miles from the proposed new town.[18] The location of the rest of the immigrants is very difficult to establish. It is unlikely that all of them were Quakers.

Samuel Starbuck (sen.) and Timothy Folger were, no doubt, the leaders. These two had control of five whaling-boats, and it is quite likely that the boats were sent to the southern seas' whaling grounds soon after unloading their human cargo. Meanwhile, Greville was anxious to begin the building of the town. He wrote to Samuel Starbuck (sen.) to tell him that a good mason and his son had been engaged and that he was to begin work immediately and '. . . in the meantime I have referred him to you for advice and to no other person'.[19] A quarry was opened for stones and a brick kiln built for the construction of new houses. The building of the town now proceeded under the direction of the Nantucketers, with Greville's approval. Timber and stone and artificers were available locally; a single wharf, or quay, was constructed and the first few houses built. But, who designed the lay-out of the streets in their gridiron pattern?

In 1797, a Frenchman, Jean Louis Barrallier, arrived in Milford.[20] He came to oversee the construction of the Naval Yard of the new town as he had acted previously in London as Assistant to the Inspector General of Naval Construction. He marked out the yard and he it was who supervised the building of ships. But Greville decided to make much wider use of Barrallier as his letter to Samuel Starbuck (sen.) (quoted in Flora Thomas' *The Builders of Milford*) implies:

I have explained to Mr Barrallier my intention to give every preference to your accommodation in my power. He has the plans of Milford . . . I have given Mr Barrallier power to open negociation [sic] with any person inclining to build which till now I could not do for want of a fixt plan . . . I do not wish a day to be lost in what he builds and as one of his sons is an architect as well as himself I have desired him to employ workmen . . .

Barrallier, therefore, would be much involved in building the town. But we are not told who drew the 'fixt plan'. Flora Thomas gives the details:

The building of the quay having been first got under way, and the Inn arranged for, other buildings were projected, and the future town began to take shape. The plan of it was on American lines. There were to be three long streets parallel with each other, and cuts down at right angles from the upper to the lower streets . . . The town was to extend to an equal distance on each side of the church, east and west . . .

The town, as we know it, has three long streets parallel with each other but

. . . the long street, Front Street [afterwards called Hamilton Terrace], lost heart ere ever it reached the site of St Cotherin's [sic] Church, and stopped considerably short, leaving a gap of open ground and trees in front of the church, and no street at all beyond it.

The Quakers had requested, from Greville, plots for building homes on the 'Front'. Daniel Starbuck leased a plot (99 years) on First Street, opposite the Custom House (at the bottom of the street now called Dartmouth).[21] Samuel Starbuck (junior) leased a piece of ground in First Street, bounded by Cross Street, east of ground occupied by Daniel Starbuck, north of Second Street. There is some evidence that the Folgers and Barralliers lived cheek by jowl in the houses now referred to as 30 and 29 Hamilton Terrace, respectively. Benjamin Rotch leased a plot and was in the process of building a house on First Street (which is now known as 25 Hamilton Terrace) but Castle Hall became vacant and he took up residence there. (The completed house on First Street was eventually used as a Bank). But some of the other immigrants built away from First Street. Samuel Starbuck (sen.) built the house now known as Priory Lodge, and nearby he built a bakery. Uriah Bunker built a large house not far from Steynton village, now known as Bunker's Hill Hotel. But we have no knowledge of where other immigrants settled.

The Quakers led a full life in Milford as described in Abial Folger's diary (1806-1811). Timothy Folger was appointed American Consul and a surveyor of ships. He also supervised the large Quaker store-house which was mainly used for storing grain—maize, barley, rye, wheat—chiefly imported from America. Samuel Starbuck (jun.) was appointed supervisor of wrecks and had control of their cargoes. One consequence of accumulation of grain at Milford was that the Quakers were able to avert famine in Pembrokeshire and in some other parts of the Principality. Daniel Starbuck was a 'merchant' and a part-time farmer; Gayer Starbuck built a brewery with the help of his father, Daniel, no doubt. The brewery was located near the present British Rail station. The Folgers kept a small holding and sold the surplus milk from their cow to neighbours.

By the time the immigrants arrived in Wales the Quaker cause was very much in decline in Pembrokeshire. Haverfordwest alone held a Meeting for Worship regularly and constituted the Monthly Meeting for the County. Daniel Starbuck was appointed its Clerk in 1794.[22] However, the Milford group held a Meeting for Worship on Sundays and Thursdays at 10 a.m. A Meeting House was built for around £500 and was used regularly from March 1811.

But, if the immigrants thought that their witness as pacifists[23] and against church tithes[24] would not be challenged, they were mistaken. They refused to pay tithes and their property was distrained; they would not be recruited to the County Militia and they were fined.

The arrival in Milford from France in 1794 of Benjamin Rotch and his family gave added impetus to the Quaker colony.[25] He owned several whaling-boats and was very wealthy. He arranged for his boats to call at Milford before proceeding to London. His financial contribution towards the building of the Meeting House was very substantial. His son Francis, together with Samuel Starbuck (jun.) and S. L. Phillips and sons of Haverfordwest opened a Bank in Milford which was known under the firm of Rotch, Phillips and Starbuck and named The Milford and Haverfordwest Bank.

According to Abial Folger's diary, the Quakers at Milford were not isolated. Many acquaintances in the whale-oil industry from Nantucket and Dartmouth (Nova Scotia) came to visit the families who had settled in Milford. Also, there seems to have been quite a traffic of Quakers to and from Ireland since the London stage-coach met the Irish Packet from Waterford at Hubberstone, Milford. Abial mentions preaching meetings which were much appreciated.

Then came a shock to the Quaker colony. In 1813 Benjamin Rotch resigned his membership of the Society:[26]

Dear Friends,

My mind being fully convinced that the withholding of tythes from those who have a legal claim to them is more criminal than paying them, I have decided to comply with all such demands but unwilling (as a member) to deviate from the Rules of the Society which I not only respect and esteem, but the fundamental principles of which I revere, I do hereby resign.

Your sincere and affectione Friend,
Benjamin Rotch

Samuel and Daniel Starbuck were appointed to confer with him, but he remained adamant.

Unfortunately, Benjamin Rotch got into financial difficulty through the carelessness of his agent in London. He was obliged to sell his house in Milford to pay his creditors. A Monthly Meeting Minute of 1817 refers to his transfer to Westminster Meeting together with a letter of recommendation to Christian Care and Oversight. (This concern about members and attenders who move to other areas is still an important feature of Quaker practice. However, in the case of Benjamin Rotch, it is unusual since he had resigned. It shows a very loving spirit towards him.)

This survey of the Quakers of the eighteenth and nineteenth centuries would not be complete without due consideration of those who made history.

There was much resentment when the Quaker whalers were persuaded to leave Dartmouth, Nova Scotia, for Wales. The Speaker of the House of Assembly wrote to the Agent for the Province in London:[27] 'This is a fatal blow aimed against the Province, and, if pursued, will be universally considered as an Act of the highest injustice . . .' The Governor of the Province of Dartmouth also wrote to the Agent: 'There is a design on foot to draw away the whole Fishery from this place to Milford Haven, which, if affected, will be the utter ruin of this Province . . . this I am persuaded would drive away many of the best settlers . . .'

Indeed, some of those who came to Milford had rendered much service in the building of Dartmouth from a wilderness to a thriving town. In 1786, as soon as he arrived in Nova Scotia,

Timothy Folger was appointed Justice of the Peace for the County of Halifax. Both Samuel Starbuck (sen.) and Timothy Folger were appointed by the House of Assembly as Trustees on the use of Common Land in Dartmouth. According to the Provincial Act of 1770, it was considered a privilege to be a Trustee and only the most dedicated, honest and responsible people could be so nominated. In 1791 Timothy Folger was appointed a Commissioner of Peace and a member of the Grand Jury, and also an Assessor for Dartmouth.

As previously stated, Samuel Starbuck (sen.) and Timothy Folger were the leaders of the immigrants to Wales. They were both past middle-age in 1792: Samuel was 64 and Timothy 60, and their wives were about the same age. Both men were well-acquainted with long sea voyages, and had experience in designing wharves, piers and stores. (It's interesting to note that the chief mate in the classic whale-hunting story 'Moby Dick', was of a line of Quakers; his name was Starbuck and hailed from Nantucket.) John Grubb of Clonmel, Ireland, who visited Milford in 1793 wrote in his diary: 'I slept [one] night in an American bed with old Sam Starbuck, a sensible man who had several years following a seafaring life in the whale fishery.'

As his letters show, Greville appointed Samuel Starbuck as correspondent for the immigrants. Samuel was of a pioneering nature, for as his whaling interests diminished he set up a bakery and a mill for grinding grain for flour. It appears that the enterprise was a great success and Greville was fascinated by the structure of both oven and mill. Samuel is commemorated in the name, Starbuck Road, near the Meeting House.

Timothy Folger was not as prominent in the civic affairs of Milford as Samuel Starbuck. This is rather surprising because Timothy had considerable talent. His cousin Benjamin Franklin, the eminent American statesman and scientist persuaded Timothy to investigate the movement of the Gulf Stream: by making use of the Stream, the voyage from America to Wales was reduced by a fortnight. On one occasion, when captaining one of his whale-boats, he was captured by the French navy and taken to France. He was offered the captaincy of one of their largest battleships. [28]

These two, Samuel Starbuck (sen.) and Timothy Folger, overshadowed the activities of the younger men in the community. Most of them were busy on whaling missions and could not play a prominent part in the affairs of Milford. But Samuel Starbuck (jun.) and Daniel, his brother, were vigorous Quakers. Daniel refused to pay church tithes and Samuel had to pay a volunteer to serve in the local militia because he refused to be enlisted. Daniel was appointed Monthly Meeting Clerk in 1794. He kept the Quaker standard that he practised as Clerk of the Dartmouth Preparative Meeting: 'marrying-out' was not tolerated and disownment followed such behaviour. The Overseers were very thorough in their concern with regard to marriage. When two members declared their intention of marrying, Overseers were appointed to visit their parents in order to ascertain that the engagement was in order and that a 'clearance notice' could be sent to Monthly Meeting. Further appointments were made for Overseers at the wedding to report it 'orderly conducted'.

Preparative Meetings in those days were subjected to queries by Monthly Meeting to which they submitted written answers. They were concerned with the behaviour of members of the Preparative Meeting and any deviations would be investigated by the Monthly Meeting.

Benjamin Rotch who came to Milford in 1794, followed later by his large family, made a considerable impact. He inspired confidence and his wealth enabled him and Elizabeth his wife to entertain Friends and others at their home on a lavish scale. During his tour of Pembrokeshire, Fenton, a well-known historian of that period, was much impressed on his visit to Castle Hall, and enjoyed a trip down the Haven in Benjamin's yacht.[29] Evidence suggests that Benjamin Rotch was most generous and kind but, as stated earlier, it seems that his wealth got in the way of his Quaker principles which led to his resignation from the Society.

Chapter 3

QUAKERS OF THE NINETEENTH AND TWENTIETH CENTURIES

During the nineteenth century the Quaker cause in Pembrokeshire continued to decline. In 1821 a Pembrokeshire Monthly Meeting minute reported that the Haverfordwest Meeting 'owing to age, infirmities and uncertain residence of others and delinquency of other members there is only one man and one woman attending the week-day Meeting'. As a result, the Meeting at Haverfordwest was discontinued and Milford Haven became the Monthly meeting for Pembrokeshire. The old Meeting Houses at Redstone and Puncheston had deteriorated very badly and were sold in 1822 and 1823, respectively. Haverfordwest Meeting House was sold sometime before 1835 because, in that year, the Shire Hall was built on the site. In 1829, a minute from Pembrokeshire Monthly Meeting held on fourth month, reads: 'The Monthly Meeting is now united with that of Carmarthen to make one Monthly Meeting.' However, by the next Monthly Meeting the union of Pembroke, Carmarthen and Glamorgan, forming South Wales Monthly Meeting, was complete.

By 1843 Quakerism in Pembrokeshire had reached a level at which it ceased to be viable. At the South Wales Monthly Meeting held at Neath on the 14th of the ninth month, 1843, minute 10 reads: 'In consequence of the death of our dear Friend, Paul Starbuck of Milford Haven, the P.M. at that place had not been held and this Meeting submits to the General Meeting that such Meeting should be discontinued.'

It is not clear from the records how the Meeting at Milford Haven operated after 1843. The Meeting was apparently discontinued in 1885, because although mentioned in the 'Book of Meetings' (an annual list of British Meetings) it is not listed as a regular meeting in the 1886 edition. It had, however, been only 'occasionally held' on 1st-day at 11 a.m., usually on the first first-day in the month since 1867, according to the 'Book of

Meetings'. In the 1886 'Book of Meetings' it appears at 11 a.m. in 1st, 2nd and 3rd months, with the rest of the year not fixed. In the Western Quarterly Meeting 'List of members' for 1875 only one member appears under Milford Haven: George Phillips (1822?-1889) of Dew Street, Haverfordwest. In his unpublished thesis (*c.* 1920), 'The Quakers of Pembrokeshire', the historian David Salmon, writes:

> Since 1800 there had not been a single member admitted 'by convincement' and I do not know of any being so admitted till 1857, when George Phillips (familiarly known as 'the Quaker' in my school-days at Haverfordwest) was received into the Society, of which he became an ornament.

In 1879, a letter appeared in *The Friend* (the Quaker weekly journal) over the name of George Phillips:

> Dear Friend,—It may, perhaps, interest some of thy readers to hear that in this remote part of South Wales we have still one meeting-house, at Milford Haven, now pretty much disused, all the members and attenders of which, with one exception, [30] are deceased. Seldom in late years have any Friends in the ministry felt drawn to visit this now solitary heritage, though in days gone by there were numerous meeting-houses and meeting-places in this county, which is still dotted over with ancient burial-grounds.
>
> In Gospel love, our dear friends, Alfred Wright of Whitby, and F. Dymond of Neath, felt it their duty to hold a series of meetings for worship in this meeting-house on the 31st of Third Month and 1st and 2nd of Fourth Month. General invitations were given and were largely responded to by a full meeting-house each evening, numbers failing to gain admission. In the ministers' gallery a clergyman and some Dissenting ministers sat beside our friends, and on the last evening the clergyman brought forward his meeting one hour to make way for the Friends' meeting. The meetings were largely owned by a divine solemnity, while the springs of Gospel ministry and supplication flowed forth freely to the edification and comfort of the people. On the last evening a meeting for

children was held at five p.m.—a season, no doubt, to be profitably remembered in after years.

All the meetings were held in simple faith on the ancient foundation of our mode of worship, and this allegiance to first principles was signally owned by the presence and power of the Master of all rightly-gathered assemblies, and to the comforting relief of the humble labourers in the spiritual vineyard.

May others be encouraged to yield in the obedience of faith to visit the waste and solitary places within our Society, and thus to comfort and strengthen that which remains.

With love, thy sincere friend,

Geo. Phillips.[31]

Fourth Month 12th 1879

His plea seems to have fallen on deaf ears. Silence fell on Milford Haven Meeting House for practically the next thirty years.

In the 'Book of Meetings' for 1906, it was announced that the Meeting House at Milford Haven was available for meetings, and in 1907, a letter initialed 'R. W.' (Richard Watkins of Swansea) appeared in *The Friend* describing his visit to Pembrokeshire. About the Meeting House at Milford Richard Watkins (the father of John Oliver Watkins, a wise treasurer of the Monthly Meeting, who died a few years ago) wrote: 'Everything within and without is neat, clean, and in good, almost perfect, repair. One hour's work (and that mainly with a duster), and the house is ready for use.' 'R. W.' was deeply moved as he walked in the Meeting House burial-ground:

We looked at the mounds, and wondered whether the dead are so dead and speechless and voiceless as we are apt to think. All was peaceful. In this calm hush, this soft quiet stillness, we verily heard voices of those that, though dead, yet speak ... What means this great silence? Why these forsaken paths? Why ascends no voice in prayer? Are there none to cry out and shout the message of gladness? If there was any virtue in the life we tried to live, come ye living ones and justify us. We who are here are not the only dead; without these walls are valleys of dead men's bones. If there is any life left in the Quaker message, come from the east, west, north and south, and in the name of the ever living One blow upon those dead bones that they may live … Looking at the sea in front of us, and the charming scenery on every hand, we thought what a place and what an opportunity for a month of splendid holiday service, a month of mission work here and now charged with wondrous possibilities.

Richard Watkins' plea seems to have reached its target. In September 1909, Western Quarterly Meeting considered

minutes from the Extension Committee, chiefly relating to the re-opened Meeting House at Milford Haven. From the last Sunday in June, we were informed, meetings had been held there, the visitors having included Herbert Sefton Jones, Sophia M. Fry, Charles Edwin Gillett, John Owen Jenkins, Alfred Young and Hercules D. Phillips, besides Richard Watkins, William George Hall and several other Friends from Swansea. Meetings have been held each Sunday morning and evening, and Bible-readings in the afternoons; and during the latter period, united meetings on Sunday evenings at 7.45 p.m. A well-attended week of meetings was held, and several Bible-readings on week-days were given and other meetings addressed by H. Sefton Jones. The population of Milford Haven has rapidly increased of late, much friendliness has been shown to Friends, and there is an excellent meeting-house, so that the Committee felt there was a call to go forward, suggesting one of two possible courses should be taken: either to continue as during the past three months, sending visitors every week; or to appeal to the Home Mission Committee, with a preference for the first proposal. This preference the Quarterly Meeting endorsed, and the Commitee was authorised to proceed.

In an account of the Western Quarterly Meeting, December 1908, it stated:

The Extension Committee reported the keeping open of the meeting-house at Milford Haven, which until the summer, save for occasional visits, had been closed for a good many years. It was stated that the recent removal of a Friend, (Sydney W. Belcher, a member of Warwickshire North Monthly Meeting) whose business engagement took him to Milford, gave a still more hopeful prospect of being able to keep the meeting open, with the help of less frequent visits.

As far as is known, Western Quarterly Meeting came to its final decision on the future of Milford Haven Meeting at Worcester in April 1909. In its report it states:

> A good deal of time was again devoted to the question of the reopened meeting at Milford Haven. The great difficulty of continuing active help and oversight, by a Quarterly Meeting Committee, of this far outlying position was strongly brought home, while on the other hand it was felt that good service had been accomplished by the numerous visitors who have gone there during the past nine or ten months. Eventually, responsibility was thrown for the next three months on the South Wales Monthly Meeting [which hitherto had shared it with Quarterly Meeting], and the Monthly Meeting was invited to report to a future meeting.

Swansea Friends, and Richard Watkins in particular, were regular visitors to the Meeting at Milford. [32] In those days, the meetings were evangelical in their approach. Many elderly Milfordians tell of happy memories at large gatherings of local children at Sunday Schools held at the meeting-house by Arthur Gwilliam, a successful draper in the town. He was attracted to the early meetings of 1908-1909, and became a member of the Society. He was active in the community, was a lay-preacher and served on the Urban District Council of which he was Chairman of the Council on at least one occasion. He had a talent for music and formed a local pipe-band. His other interest was the Rechabite movement and he attained a high level of office as a Good Templar.

Arthur was Correspondent of the Meeting when we came to know him in 1949. And, since he had built four houses, two on either side of the Meeting-house, and because he lived in one of them, he was acting-warden of the Quaker property.

By 1949, there was little activity within the Meeting-house. Gone were the Sunday Schools, but hymns and choruses by Sankey and Moody were sung at Meeting for Worship every First day from a publication, of which there were abundant copies in the Meeting. But, since hymns and choruses need a reasonably large congregation, the performance at Meeting for Worship was not inspiring. There were seldom more than six present and often as few as two. In winter, we used to huddle round the fireplace at one end of the long room which was difficult to keep warm, while the children went for Sunday-school to Arthur Gwilliam's house.

Very slowly, the Meeting gathered momentum. A family of vigorous Quakers from Lancashire[33] came to live next door to the Meeting House and a family with small children moved into the area from the north of Pembrokeshire.[34] Waldo Williams, a local pacifist, also applied for membership. By 1954, we felt confident enough in the future prosperity of the Meeting to apply for the status of Preparative Meeting. Arthur Gwilliam was appointed Clerk; we were glad of the opportunity to thank him for his many years of devotion to the Society and his care of the Meeting-House which he never allowed to close its doors.

A new spirit was taking hold. Members laboured at improving the Meeting House, and replaced the old roof. John Hoyland[35] brought a group of young people from Woodbroke, (a Quaker Centre in Birmingham) to re-decorate the interior. Work parties were organized to improve the environment, including the burial-ground. John Oliver Watkins kept an eye on our progress and became treasurer of the appeal committee when we decided to build an annexe which could be used for the children's class, for tea-parties, including Monthly Meeting tea, and for a holiday centre for Friends. Now it is used five days a week by a pre-school playgroup.

In 1969, South Wales Monthly Meeting was held at Milford Haven; the first Monthly Meeting in Pembrokeshire since 1829.

A closer relationship with Monthly Meeting has been very helpful especially so when one member became Monthly Meeting Clerk. A Monthly Meeting Family Gathering over a weekend at a Friend's hotel at Tenby became an annual event and the Meeting became less isolated. But isolation cannot be completely overcome since Milford is about seventy miles from the nearest Preparative Meetings. The Meeting is isolated even from its own members and attenders, there being only one member living in the town and other members and attenders scattered over distances up to twenty miles. Members living beyond twenty miles away, such as those in the St. Davids, north Pembrokeshire and Carmarthen areas were encouraged to establish Meetings of their own. But they need more support. Monthly Meeting projects such as the *Quaker Newsletter* are helpful in this respect.

In recent years, members have taken more interest in the Milford Haven Council of Churches. In 1989 four sessions were held including three workshops, on the theme of Justice, Peace and the Integrity of Creation. Representatives of local churches, including a vicar and two United Reform ministers, came to the Meeting House. It is hoped to deepen this relationship.

One major national project which has brought members, attenders and children together is the creation of a tapestry panel (illustrated on the front cover) based on the theme 'Live Adventurously'. It depicts the arrival in Milford of the Quaker Whalers in 1792. Their adventurous living began with a refusal to take part in a war; the panel has been extended to include similar witness by one member, Waldo Williams, who served two periods of imprisonment for withholding tax in protest against the waste and inhumanity of war. As Waldo was a prominent Welsh poet, lines from one of his poems, with an English translation appear on the tapestry:

> Blest is the generation that hears them,
> The Peacemakers, the children of God.

'Living Adventurously' is not meant to be a slogan but a way of life. The Quaker Tapestry is an inspiring tribute to the lives of local Quakers who strove, in their own way, to establish the Kingdom of God on Earth, and in 1990 it became part of an exhibition of 75 panels displayed in the Festival Hall, and subsequently beside the Bayeux Tapestry in France.

References

1 Swarthmore MSS.

2 George Fox Journal.

3 Glamorgan Archives, Cardiff, documents DSF.

4 Richard Davies, 'An account of the convincement, exercises, services and travels of Richard Davies', publ. London, 1840, or a Welsh translation publ. Philadelphia, 1877.

5 'The Quakers of Pembrokeshire', David Salmon c. 1920, unpublished.

6 ibid.

7 Collection of the sufferings, publ. in two volumes by the Society of Friends.

8 'The Quakers of Pembrokeshire', ibid.

9 ibid.

10 Crynwyr Bore Cymru 1653-1659, Richard Jones, 1931.

11 Welsh Founders of Pennsylvania (Glenn) quoted by David Salmon in 'The Quakers of Pembrokeshire', ibid.

12 'The Quakers of Pembrokeshire', ibid.

13 The Story of Milford, J. F. Rees, pub. University of Wales, 1954.

14 Nantucket Island, Robert Gambee, publ. W. W. Norton & Co., New York and London.

15 Whales and Destiny, Edouard A. Stackpole, publ. University of Massachussetts Press, 1972.

16 The Starbuck papers—ref D/BT—Historical Archives, Haverfordwest.

17 Whales and Destiny, ibid.

18 Life of Mary Dudley, Elizabeth Dudley, publ. London, 1825.

19 The Builders of Milford, Flora Thomas, publ. The Western Telegraph, Haverfordwest, (reprint, 1952).

20 The Story of Milford, ibid.

21 The Starbuck papers, ibid.

22 Pembrokeshire Monthly Meeting minute.

23 Report from Pembrokeshire Monthly Meeting 5/1st month/1797: 'Sam. Starbuck (jun.) had taken from his by warrant and distraint £10 to pay for a substitute to the Supplementary Militia, he having been drawn by ballot to serve the said Militia.'

24 Daniel Starbuck's refusal to pay church tithes: Copy of Warrants in Appendix 6.

25 The Builders of Milford, ibid.

26 Minute of Pembrokeshire Monthly Meeting.

27 The History of the Dartmouth Quakers, Douglas Wm. Trider.

28 Nantucket Island, ibid.

29 Historical Tour through Pembrokeshire, Richard Fenton, 1811.

30 Eleanor Starbuck, the widow of Gayer Starbuck died in 1879, age 79.

31 George Phillips was buried, 1889, in the Haverfordwest cemetery.

32 Arthur Gwilliam of Milford Haven Meeting often mentioned the visits of Richard Watkins to the Meeting House.

33 William and Edith Whitworth, Ann and Jennifer. Clemency and Stephen Griffith with Dilys, Margaret (and later Enid) were there since 1949.

34 Winnie and James Kilroy, Alice and Kathleen.

35 A tutor at Woodbroke.

Appendix 1

EMIGRANTS TO PENNSYLVANIA (c.1682-1711)

This list is taken from an incomplete catalogue by Glenn, entitled *Welsh Founders of Pennsylvania* (figures in bracket denote year of emigration).

Haverfordwest: Janet Humphries, a servant to George Painter (1683); George Painter (1683); David Jones, bailiff (1700); Francis Lloyd, shoemaker (1686); Samuel Jones (or John) (1709).

Llanddewi Felffre: Lewis David, gentleman, (1690), but leaving some of his children in Wales; Rees Hent, farmer (1688), he returned to fetch his family in 1694; Alice Lewis (1710) and her brother John Lewis, farmer (1710); John Rice, a minor, son of David Rice, (1696) with the consent of his parents.

Narberth: John Scourfield, gentleman, son and heir of Maurice Scourfield—one of the first to buy land in Pennsylvania. Date of emigration not recorded.

Redstone: Thomas Ellis (1683); Francis Jones (1711); Daniel Lewis (1701/2); Henry Lewis, gentleman, (1682/3), married Margaret Protheroe 1670.

Tenby: William Jenkins, emasculator, born 1648, married in 1678 Elizabeth, daughter of Lewis Griffith of Tenby, (1685) died 1712.

[Jameston: John Skone, 1727]

Puncheston: David Lawrence (1683) with Thomas Ellis, whose daughter he married.

Castlebythe: William Howel (c.1683); Maurice Llewelyn, gentleman (1686), born 1645.

Llandisilio: Francis Howel (1684), married to Margaret Mortimer, died 1696.

Uzmaston: John Hayes, husbandman, son of Richard Hayes sen. (1687); Richard Hayes sen., farmer (1687), died at an advanced age, 1697; Richard Hayes jun., farmer (1687), son of Richard Hayes sen., married Elizabeth, daughter of Henry Lewis of Redstone, died 1738.

Little Newcastle: Morgan David, farmer (before 1694).

Bayvil: James Rowland, gentleman, of Rhos y Bayvil (1700).

The following are simply said to be of 'County Pembroke': Griffith Jones, a minister (1709), born 1683 died 1778; John Lewis, farmer (1683) died 1704; Thomas Owen, farmer, (before 1692); Philip Price, bailiff, (before 1692); Owen Thomas came to Pennsylvania on a visit in 1710, and is supposed to have stayed; Simeon Thomas, bailiff (1708)

Appendix 2

THE SUFFERERS

No dates are given for imprisonment in Haverfordwest. The following were certainly residents of the County of Pembroke:

Haverfordwest: William Bateman and his wife Sarah; Evan Bowen (Prendergast); John Burge; Mary Eddowe; Morgan Eynon, and Joan his wife; James Jones; Francis Lloyd (Prendergast); Hugh Lloyd; Catherine Lockyer; Elizabeth Luntly; Peregrine Musgrave; Henry Relief and Elizabeth his wife; James Thomas; Nell Woolford.
Rudbaxton: Edward Lord.
Llanddewi Felffre: Lewis David and Susan, his wife; Evan John; Alice Lewis; James Lewis; David Rice.
Llawhaden: William Thomas.
Narberth: John Husband; Evan Protheroe.
Redstone: Thomas Ellis; Henry Lewis.
Robeston Wathen: Harry Lewis; John Poyer.
Tenby: David Hitchins; William Jenkins; James Lewis; (Thomas Barrett is mentioned as a Friend living here in 1659).
Puncheston: David Lawrence; Thomas Simmons and Jane, his wife, and their sons, Hugh, John and Evan.
Henry's Moat: Evan Simmons (the son of Thomas and Jane Simmons?)
Spittal: William Owen.
Castlebythe: Maurice Llewelyn; Mary Llewelyn.
Wiston: James James.
Llandisilio: Richard Evan; George Lewis.
Llanycefn: Thomas Griffith.
Llangolman: Lewis James.
Uzmaston: Richard Hayes.
Reynalton: Thomas Willis.
Hacket: (near Reynalton): John Harris.

Besse, the London-based recorder of the Sufferers does not say where the following lived, but as they were imprisoned at Haverfordwest it can be assumed that they lived in Pembrokeshire, except when it was known that they were visitors: Henry Clayton; Robert Cornock; Thomas David; John Davis; David Edward; Henry Edward; Laurence Edward; Margaret Edward; Henry Evan; William Fortune; Abigail (the wife of William Gray); Howel Griffith; Rice Harris; John Hilline; John Holme(s); Elizabeth Howel; John Howel; Thomas Kent; James Lewis; John Lewis; Griffith Morgan; Maurice Owen; Philip Price; David Simmons; Francis Simmons; Ursula Simmons; Richard White; Thomas William; David Williams; Edmund Williams; Humphrey Williams and Rebecca (his wife); Rebecca Williams, junior.
Visitors: Alice Birkett; Elizabeth Holme; John Holme; James Picton; Richard Poole.
The following probably lived in the County: Maurice Cole; John Evans; Edward Griffith; John Griffith; Joseph Griffith; William Hillay; David Jones; Griffith Jones; Owen Lewis.
The following possibly lived in the County: Arthur Bewes; Amos Davies; Evan Davies; Rice Evans; Maurice Humphrey; Elizabeth John; Morgan John; Susan Mansell; John Meredith; Pierce Morris; Philip Price; John Reynolds; William Reynolds; John Richards; Ellis Roberts; John Robins; John Williams.

Appendix 3

TOMBSTONES IN MILFORD HAVEN MEETING HOUSE GRAVEYARD

	Date of Burial	Age
Abigail Starbuck, wife of Samuel Starbuck (sen.)	1801	
Samuel Starbuck (sen.) arrived Milford August 1792	1803	75
Benjamin Starbuck, son of Samuel Starbuck (jun.)	1810	19 years
Annie Starbuck	1810	5 months
Timothy Folger, arrived Milford August 1792	1814	82 years
Abial Folger, wife of Timothy	1816	80 years
Daniel Starbuck, son of Samuel Starbuck, arrived Milford Haven June 1792	1818	67 years
W. F. H. O(wen), probably the son of William Owen	1818	5 years
Lucretia Starbuck, wife of Samuel Starbuck (jun.) and daughter of Abial and Timothy Folger	1821	59 years
Alice Starbuck, wife of Daniel Starbuck	1822	
W. O(wen) kept a hotel at Hubberstone connected with the Irish 'packet'	1826	57 years
Samuel Starbuck (jun.)	1829	67 years
Paul Starbuck, son of Daniel Starbuck	1843	
Alice Starbuck, daughter of Daniel Starbuck	1844	
C.A.H.B. These are the children of	1849	18 months
A.B. Robert Hill Butcher of London	1850	4 months
A.R.J.B. and of Sophia, his wife,	1851	4 months
F.H.B. of Penmynydd or Llanfynydd,	1852	3 weeks
R.H.O.B. Carmarthenshire	1854	3 months
Margaret Morgan	1856	16 years
F. O. (Fanny Owen), probably wife of Wm. Owen	1857	85 years
J. A. (Jane Allen?), in same grave as F. O.	1862	65 years
Gayer Starbuck, son of Daniel Starbuck	1858	77 years
Mary Starbuck, widow of Paul	1862	

	Date of Burial	Age
Sarah Starbuck, daughter of Samuel Starbuck (jun.)	1863	
William Gayer Starbuck, son of Samuel Starbuck (jun.)	1865	54 years
Elizabeth Starbuck, wife of Alfred Barrett Starbuck	1869	
Richard Penrose Starbuck, son of Gayer Starbuck	1872	38 years
Guy Griffith, son of George and Mary Griffith, great grand-child of Daniel Starbuck whose grand-daughter married a Dr Billy Griffith, who is still known in Milford Haven	1872	9 months
Alfred Bassett Starbuck, son of Paul Starbuck	1874	
Esther Garrett	1874	60 years
Fanny Fenwick	1877	77 years
Eleanor Starbuck, widow of Gayer Starbuck	1879	79 years
William Garrett, husband of Esther	1887	69 years
Mary Ann Adams	1908	74 years

Two small tombstones—RPS and GS—not identified. Abial Folger, in her diary, mentions other burials but they are without tombstones.

38

Appendix 4

THE MORE PROMINENT OF THE QUAKER FAMILIES WHO CAME TO MILFORD HAVEN FROM AMERICA

The Starbucks

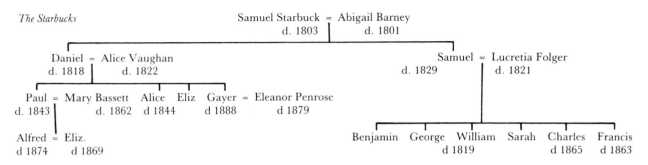

The Folgers

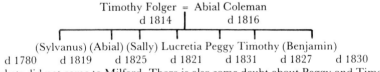

Those in brackets did not come to Milford. There is also some doubt about Peggy and Timothy (Jun.).

The Rotches

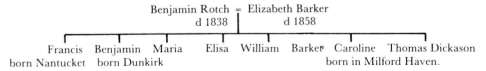

The family grave is in Kensal Green Cemetery, London

Appendix 5

INFORMATION ABOUT SOME OF THE LESS PROMINENT IMMIGRANTS OF 1792

Captain Charles Gardner died in Natucket in 1848, age 79 years.

Judith Bunker died in Nantucket in 1831 (age 83 years). William, the son of Judith and Zacchary, died in Liverpool; their other children left Milford but did not return to Nantucket.

Ruth Bunker died in Nantucket in 1831, age 38.

David Grieve, husband of Peggy (Folger) is mentioned in *Builders of Milford* (p. 36) being referred to by Greville as a 'good and ingenious young man', whose plans Greville would be glad to promote. Were David and Peggy immigrants to Milford then? If so, they did not stay. They were buried in Providence, Rhode Island.

Captain Gwinn had his base in New Bedford, U.S.A. (where he is possibly buried); he was a frequent visitor to Milford after his first voyage in 1792.

Captain Uriel Bunker was buried in Steynton, near Milford, in 1841 aged 64 years.

Timothy Folger (Jun.) died Nantucket, 1827.

SUMMONS AND INVENTORY OF GOODS DISTRAINED FROM DANIEL STARBUCK, 1811

[No. 64.]

R. B.

Pembrokeshire
To wit

} WHEREAS Complaint hath been made unto us *Henry Leach and Anthony Stokes Esquires*

two of his Majesty's Justices of the Peace for the said *County.*
by *Willm Powell of Ford servant to the Wrights of iron of Haverfordwest*
that *~~the several Persons hereunder mentioned~~* being Persons commonly called Quakers, have refused to pay to, or to compound with, him the said *Willm Powell on behalf of the Wrights* for ~~their~~ Tythes and other Rights, Dues, and Payments, belonging to the Church of *Slainston in the said County* ————— and justly due unto ~~him~~ the said *the Wrights* ————— ————— We therefore the said Justices, being neither of us Patron of the Parish Church of *Slainston* ————— aforesaid, nor any way interested in any

41

of the said Tythes, Rights, Dues, or other Payments, having duly summoned the said ~~several Persons~~ *Daniel Norbick* before us, and having also duly examined the Truth of the said Complaint upon Oath, do find that there are justly due for the same from the said several Persons respectively, to ~~him~~ the said *Am Wright* — — — — — — — — — the several and respective Sums hereunder specified; and do order and appoint the said ~~several Persons~~ *Daniel Norbick* respectively, to pay or cause to be paid unto ~~him~~ the said *Am Wright* — — — — — — — — the said several and respective Sums. And we do also order and appoint the said ~~several Persons~~ *Daniel Norbick* to pay, or cause to be paid, unto ~~him~~ the said *Am Wright* — — — — — — the further several and respective Sums hereunder specified, for such Costs and Charges concerning the Premises, as upon the Merits of the Cause do appear to us just and reasonable. Given under our Hands and Seals at *Melford* — in the said *County* — the *Seventh* — Day of *December* — in the Year of our Lord *1811*

Ant Stokes

W. Cooke

Sold by COLES, DUNN, and KNIGHT, Stationers, No. 21, Fleet Street.

} To the Constable of the parish ——— of Staunton
in the said County

R. B.

WHEREAS *William Purcell of Ford servant to Mrs Ann Wright of Maror for Guest* ——— hath complained unto us *Henry Lucch and Anthony Stokes, Esqrs* two of his Majesty's Justices of the Peace for the said *County* ——— that *Daniel Starbuck of the town of Milford in the parish of Staunton in the said County, Merchant*

being Person commonly called Quakers, have refused to pay unto him the said *Walter Purcell on behalf of Ann Wright* or to compound for the Tythes and other Rights, Dues, and Payments, belonging to the Church of *Staunton in the said County* ——— and justly due from them to him the said *Ann Wright* ——— These are therefore to authorize and require you forthwith to summon the said several Persons to appear before us at *the Coopers Arms* in *the town of Milford* ——— in the said *County* ——— on *Saturday* ——— the *Seventh* Day of *December last* at the Hour of *One O'Clock* in the *afternoon* of the same Day, to answer unto the said Complaint. And be you then there to certify what you shall have done in the Premises. Given under our Hands and Seals at *Milford* — in the said *County* the *Seventh* Day of *December* in the Year of our Lord *1811*

Daniel Starbuck

1811

Sold by COLES, KN'd DUNN, No. 21, Fleet Street

PRINTED BY L. COLD, SHOE-LANE, LONDON.

43

An Inventory of the several goods and chattels Distrained by the
Thomas Venables being a constable of and in the parish of Stainton the
Twelfth day of Sept 1811 in the field of Mr Daniel Starbuck Situated
Between Priory and Milford in the parish of Stainton in the county of Pembroke
By the authority of a warrant under the hands & seals H Leach & A J Stokes Esqrs being
the to nearest Magistrates within the said county and in the behalf of Mrs
An Wright the Impropriator of tythes due on the said premises for three pounds
Fower shillings being to years tythes due Michelmas day last for the premises
And as yet in arear and unpaid —————————————————

In ye above Field a Cut of Hay at the west
End of the the rick to a cut Mark on each side
of the rick from Cut to cut right across the rick

Appraised at ————————————————— £5 : 0 : 0

44

Mr Daniel Starbuck Take Notice that I as Constable to ye above mentioned
Justices have this day Distrained the goods and chattels mentioned in the above inventory
For the sum of 3:4:0 being to years tythes due Michelmas day last for the premises above
Mentioned and have deemed the said goods & Chattels on the premises as pr Inventory
And that unless the said arrears of tythes and discharges of this distres are paid on the
goods and chattels replevied within fower days from the date hereof the
said goods will be appraised and sold to law.
Dated at Milford the 12 Day of Decbr 1811   Jno Turner Constable

Milford 12 Decbr 1811 Recd of James Eaves
The sum of five pounds for ye above out of Hay
As pr Inventory   By the Jno Turner

Account of the Expences Incured
for the process in 1811 Mr Wm Farrell 4 Journeys to milford
In order to obtain Judicia advice 0:10:0
for serving the summon to Newcame 0:1:0
for serving the order of payment 0:2:0
totale first year 0:13:0

for reppetition
in 1812   To Mr Wm Farrell ———— 0:10:0
To summons ———————— 0:1:0
To order ————————— 0:2:0

Executing and swearing apprais
And seling ye distress 0:7:0

totale both years 1:13:0

amount of tythes 3:4:0

£ 4:18:0

46

ADDENDUM TO 3RD IMPRESSION.

Page 36. Appendix 2. The Sufferers.
ADD Jameston Meeting – James Skone

Page 37 Appendix 3. Tombstones.
The missing ages in the list of graves are: Abigail Starbuck 71, Alice Starbuck 67, Paul Starbuck 65, Alice Starbuck (wife of Daniel) 61, Mary Starbuck 75.

Continued on Page 38
Sarah Starbuck 72, Elizabeth Starbuck 60, Alfred Starbuck 56.

Page 39 Appendix 4   The Rotches
The names of Maria and Elisa should be reversed and places of birth should be deleted.